MEGASTRUCTURES

THE LONGEST BRIDGES

by Susan K. Mitchell

Gareth Stevens Publishing

Please visit our web site at: www.garethstevens.com
For a free color catalog describing Gareth Stevens Publishing's list of high-quality books, call 1-800-542-2595 (USA) or 1-800-387-3178 (Canada).

Library of Congress Cataloging-in-Publication Data

Mitchell, Susan K.
The longest bridges / by Susan K. Mitchell.
p. cm. — (Megastructures)
Includes bibliographical references and index.
ISBN-10: 0-8368-8364-0 (lib. bdg.)
ISBN-13: 978-0-8368-8364-0 (lib. bdg.)
1. Bridges—Juvenile literature. 2. World records—Juvenile literature. I. Title.
TG148.M58 2008
624.2—dc22 2007007098

This edition first published in 2008 by
Gareth Stevens Publishing
A Weekly Reader® Company
1 Reader's Digest Road
Pleasantville, NY 10570-7000 USA

Editorial direction: Mark J. Sachner
Editor: Barbara Kiely Miller
Art direction and design: Tammy West
Picture research: Diane Laska-Swanke
Production: Jessica Yanke
Illustrations: Spectrum Creative Inc.

Picture credits: Cover, title, p. 24 © AFP/Getty Images; p. 5 © Skip Nall/CORBIS; p. 7 © Colin Garratt; Milepost 92 1/2/CORBIS; p. 10 © Bettmann/CORBIS; pp. 12-13 © Gabriel Bouys/AFP/Getty Images; p. 15 © Mark E. Gibson/CORBIS; p. 17 © John Howard; Cordaiy Photo Library Ltd./CORBIS; p. 19 © Enzo & Paolo Ragazzini/CORBIS; pp. 20-21 © Francis Dean/Getty Images; pp. 26, 27 © AP Images; p. 29 © Pat O'Hara/CORBIS

Printed in the United States of America

1 2 3 4 5 6 7 8 9 11 10 09 08 07

CONTENTS

On the Cover: The water under the Akashi Kaikyo bridge – the world's longest suspension bridge – was calm enough for sailboats on the day this photo was taken. The water is often rough and dangerous, however.

BRIDGING THE GAPS

The Lake Pontchartrain (pon chur-train) Causeway in southern Louisiana is an incredible bridge. It stretches more than 20 miles (32 kilometers). The bridge is so long, if someone stood in the center he or she could not see land on either end. This amazing length, however, does not make it the longest bridge in the world.

Bridges are measured by their spans, not their total distance. The span is the distance of a bridge between two supports. The Pontchartrain Causeway uses hundreds of small spans. Each 100-foot- (30-meter-) long span is held up by concrete piers, which are vertical supports.

The current "World's Longest Bridge" is the Akashi Kaikyo in Japan. Its main span is more than six hundred times longer than one of the Causeway's small spans! The total distance of the Akashi Kaikyo is much shorter than the Pontchartrain Causeway. The unbelievable length of its main span, however, earns it the title of the longest bridge in the world.

Bridge Basics

There are four main kinds of bridges. A beam bridge has the simplest design. A single surface, or deck, is supported on each end by land or piers. The piers support all the weight of the bridge. Most beam bridges can reach only 200 feet (61 m) long. If they were any longer, they would not be strong enough in the middle. They would snap in two! Most of the bridges in the United States are beam bridges.

An arch bridge is strong because of its unique design. The arch bridge does not put all of its weight on piers. The curved arch takes the pressure and spreads it evenly over the entire bridge. In ancient Rome, people built arch bridges using nothing more than

Twisted vine and rope bridges like this one can still be found in forests all over the world.

Nature's Bridges

Without bridges, early travelers often had to go a long way to get across water or a deep valley. Fallen trees were some of the first natural bridges. Time and rushing water carved some stone structures into bridges, too. They took thousands of years to form.

Many early people made bridges from vines. They twisted vines together and stretched them across rivers. In places without vines, people wove grasses and roots into ropes. No matter what blocked their paths, people have been determined to find ways around the obstacles!

cut stones. Today, people build arch bridges from steel or super strong concrete. Modern arch bridges can reach more than 1,300 feet (396 m) long.

Cantilever bridges are like beam bridges but with a few changes. A cantilever bridge uses balance to support itself. One end is anchored to a riverbank or piece of land. It keeps the other end balanced and straight, much like a diving board. Some cantilever sections are built using piers. These sections are shaped like the letter "T," with each pier having two "arms." One piece of the deck is added to each arm at the same time to keep the cantilever balanced. Builders can connect several balanced cantilever sections together by putting smaller sections between them. The longest cantilever bridge is in Québec, Canada. It is 1,800 feet (549 m) long.

BALANCED CANTILEVER BRIDGE CONSTRUCTION

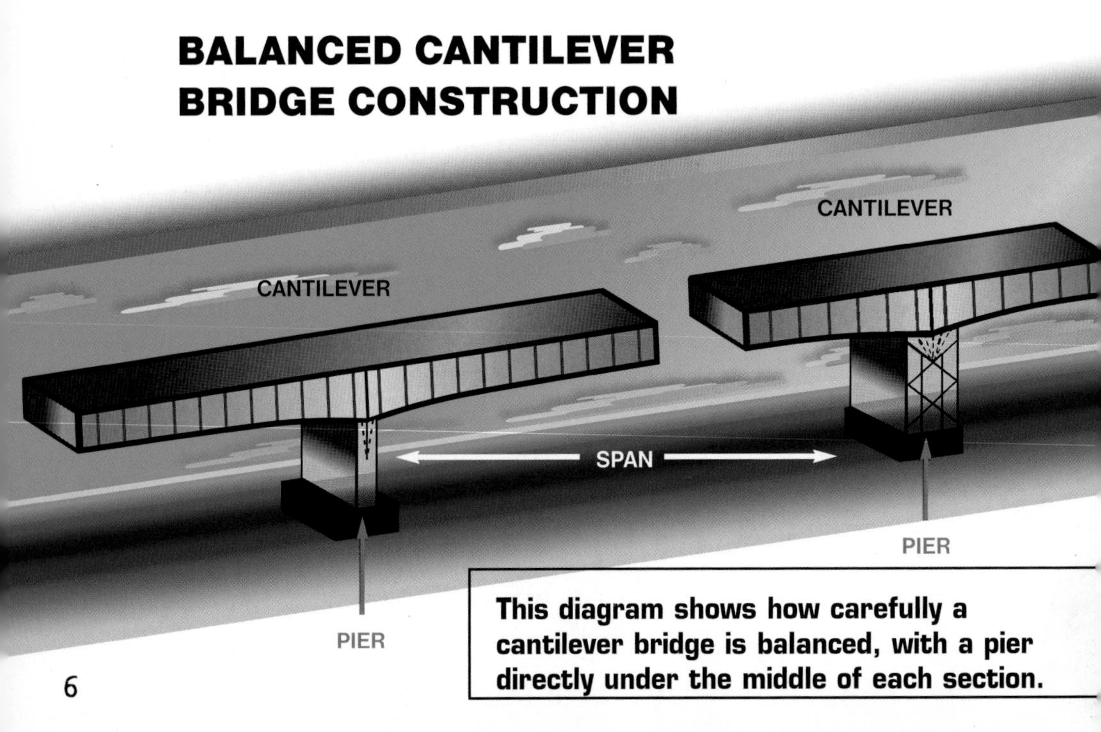

This diagram shows how carefully a cantilever bridge is balanced, with a pier directly under the middle of each section.

The Firth of Forth Bridge in Scotland is a good example of a cantilever bridge. Steel tubes coming from the top and bottom of the towers help support the cantilever arms.

The Longest of the Long

Steel suspension bridges have the longest spans in the world. These amazing structures can be identified by their swooping cables and tall towers. Because cables hold up the bridge decks, suspension bridges can cover long distances with fewer supports. Several steel strands are twisted together to make up the main cables of a suspension bridge. Hundreds of individual steel wires are twisted together to make up each strand. The main cables are incredibly strong. They help support the several thousand tons of concrete and steel that make up a bridge deck.

Two main cables are draped over soaring support towers. Workers attach the ends of each main cable to anchorages on both ends of the bridge. Other cables, called hangers or suspenders, hang straight down from the main cables and connect to the deck. Together, the towers and cables support the bridge.

No one really knows how long a suspension bridge can reach. Plans have been made to build a

A suspension bridge receives strength and support from several places — the cables, the anchorages, and the support piers.

huge bridge to join the island of Sicily to the rest of Italy. When finished, it would have a span of almost 2 miles (3 km). With bridges continuing to reach such amazing lengths, travel over water becomes much easier.

MEGA FACTS

Bridges have to be strong enough to support both "dead" and "live" loads. The dead load is the weight of the bridge itself when empty. The live load includes the bridge plus the traffic that crosses it, such as cars, people, and trains.

CHAPTER 2

GATEWAY TO THE BAY

The Golden Gate Bridge crosses the Golden Gate Strait in San Francisco, California. The strait is where the choppy waters of the Pacific Ocean meet San Francisco Bay. In the early 1900s, the only way to cross the strait was by ferry. It was often a slow and risky trip. At times, the strait was foggy and the waters were rough. Building a bridge across the strait would be very difficult.

Bridge designer Joseph Strauss took on the challenge. He finished plans for a massive bridge in 1921. It had both a cantilever and suspension design. Many people worried about how much the bridge would cost. Others doubted that Strauss could build a bridge in such dangerous waters. Some people filed lawsuits to stop Strauss from building a bridge.

Joseph Strauss fought for his bridge in court and won. Construction of the Golden Gate Bridge began on January 5, 1933. During the long court battles, Strauss hired an engineer named Charles A. Ellis. Ellis took Strauss's original design and changed it. He turned it into the long suspension bridge that now connects San Francisco with the Golden Gate National Recreation Area and communities of Marin County.

Lessons from Galloping Gertie

The Golden Gate Bridge has been a structural success. Not all bridges have been so lucky. The Tacoma Narrows Bridge in Washington State was a 1-mile- (1.6-km-) long suspension bridge built in 1940. Engineers designed the bridge to move with the wind.

Unfortunately, the bridge twisted too much. It was nicknamed "Galloping Gertie." On November 7, 1940, the bridge whipped around in the wind so wildly that it eventually ripped itself apart. Support cables snapped and the bridge crashed into the river below. Luckily, all the people on the bridge were able to get out of their cars and off the bridge before it collapsed.

Bridge builders studied the accident and learned better methods of designing and building bridges. A new bridge opened in 1951, but an even newer Tacoma Narrows Bridge should be completed in 2007.

The tangled and twisted remains of the Tacoma Narrows Bridge hung from where a section of the deck collapsed into Puget Sound in 1940.

Bombs Away

The north pier of the bridge was pretty simple to build. Its foundation was built in the shallow water at the edge of a cliff. The south pier was more difficult. Workers had to build it 1,100 feet (335 m) from the shore. The currents there were fast and rough. Digging the enormous hole for the south pier's foundation was tricky.

Workers on a barge dropped small bombs in the water to blow holes in the strait's floor. Then they carefully lowered larger bombs loaded with 200 pounds (91 kilograms) of dynamite into the holes.

Divers did all the work underwater. They searched in the dark waters to find wires attached to these larger bombs. The divers then swam the wires back up to a barge. Once on the barge, workers fastened the wires to a detonator, which would set off the bombs. Workers moved the barge out of the way and detonated the large bombs. The explosion created a football-field-sized crater where workers built the south pier and its fender. The fender was a giant concrete ring that protected the workers who built the pier from the dangerous waters of the strait.

Making History

While workers started on the south pier of the Golden Gate Bridge, its north tower headed skyward. By June 1935, builders had completed both towers. The towers reached 746 feet (227 m) tall. After the

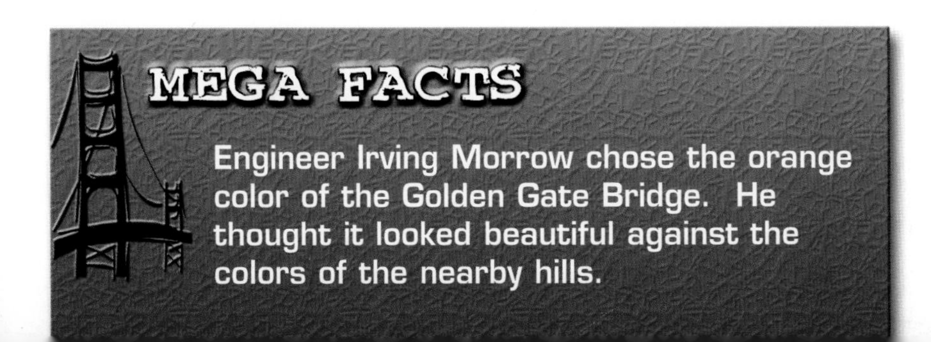

towers were complete, workers had to hang the cables.

Today, machines do most of the work of spinning wire strands into cables. In the 1930s, people did that job. They worked on high walkways in the strong winds that blow in from the Pacific Ocean. Workers laid the last wire strand on May 20, 1936. They used a special machine to squeeze the wire strand bundles into main cables 3 feet (1 m) thick. The cables are held together by large wire bands.

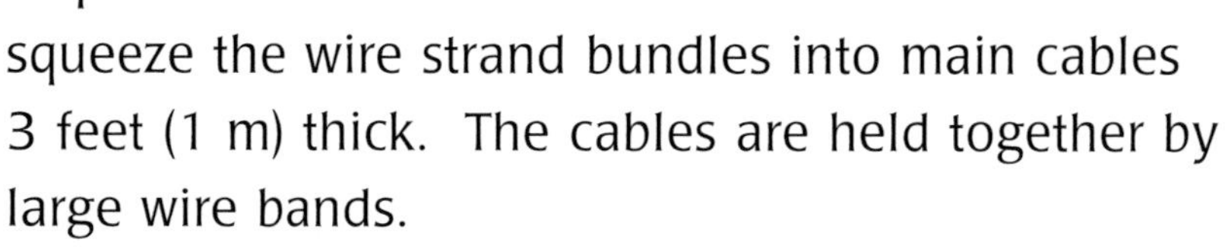

Workers then hung vertical hanger cables along the main cable. Large cranes lifted the bridge deck into place 220 feet (67 m) above the water. The deck

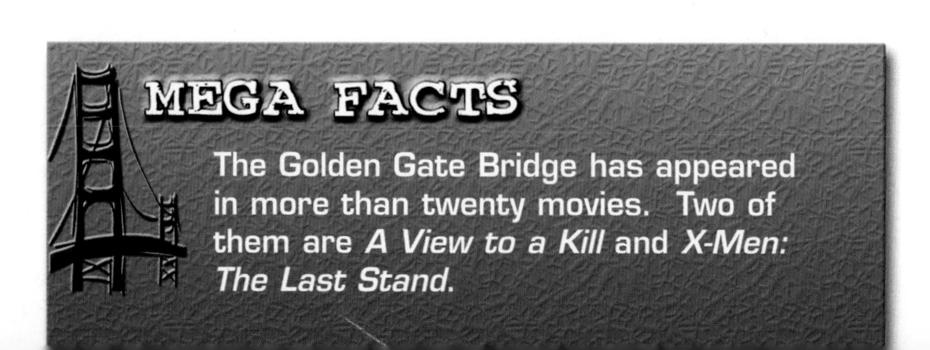

Its brillant orange color and scenic location help make the Golden Gate Bridge possibly one of the most photographed bridges in the world.

was placed high enough to allow ships to easily pass beneath the bridge. Bit by bit, workers pieced the bridge together. When the Golden Gate Bridge was finished in April 1937, it became the world's longest bridge. Its main span stretched a record-breaking 4,200 feet (1,280 m).

Sixty Feet Wins the Title

In 1964, the Golden Gate Bridge lost its place as the world's longest bridge. That year, the Verrazano Narrows Bridge opened in New York City. It took over the title by being only 60 feet (18 m) longer than the Golden Gate Bridge.

City officials named the bridge for explorer Giovanni de Verrazano, who was the first European to see the New York Harbor in 1524. The height of the bridge deck changes with the seasons. Because steel cables expand in hot temperatures, the cables are longer in the summer and the bridge deck is 12 feet (3.5 m) lower then.

CHAPTER 3

CROSSING THE HUMBER

The longest bridge in Great Britain is the Humber Bridge. Its main span stretches an incredible 4,626 feet (1,410 m). It crosses the Humber Estuary near the busy port city of Hull. The Humber Bridge held the title of World's Longest Bridge for more than sixteen years.

British merchants first came up with a plan to cross the Humber Estuary in 1872. They were unhappy with the ferry service and wanted to build a tunnel. Many plans after that came and went, but none of them resulted in a bridge being built. The British government finally approved a plan for a suspension bridge in 1959. Construction did not actually begin, however, until 1973.

On Sinking Sands

The biggest challenge in building a bridge across the Humber Estuary was at the bottom of the estuary

MEGA FACTS

Bridge designers tested a model of the Humber Bridge in a wind tunnel before building it. They had to make sure strong winds would not cause movements that would rip apart the bridge.

The famed London Bridge (*shown in Arizona*) inspired the nursery rhyme "London Bridge is Falling Down."

itself. The sands on the river floor are constantly shifting. Because this causes the depth of the river to change in certain places, ships often have to change paths to avoid getting stuck on the sand. With only one tall tower at each end, a suspension bridge would give ships enough room to change course under the bridge.

The second problem to conquer was the geology of the area. The north bank of the estuary was solid chalk. It was firm enough for workers to anchor the north tower of the bridge directly into the bank.

Where London Bridge Lives Now

London Bridge was one of the oldest bridges in the world. In A.D. 60, ancient Romans first used wood to build the bridge. It has been changed many times. A stone bridge replaced the original wooden bridge in 1209.

Bridge designer John Rennie replaced that bridge with a granite, five-arched bridge in 1831. That bridge, however, began to sink. In 1968, a new concrete bridge replaced it. The concrete bridge still stands over the Thames River in England.

A United States businessman bought Rennie's granite London Bridge. The bridge was shipped to the United States in numbered sections. Workers then rebuilt the famous London Bridge over Lake Havasu in Arizona.

Workers had to build the south tower in the river itself, however, because the south bank was made of soft clay. To support the south tower, a giant concrete anchorage was built on the south bank. It weighed more than 300,000 tons (270,000 tonnes).

Workers draped two enormous main cables over the 500-foot (152-m) towers. More than fourteen thousand wires bundled together made up each cable. After workers put the main cables in place, they attached vertical cables to support the bridge deck. Barges floated 124 giant deck sections out onto the river. Each section weighed about 140 tons (130 tonnes). Then giant cranes lifted each deck section so it could be welded into place.

No Free Ride

The Humber Bridge opened for traffic on June 24, 1981. Money to build the bridge was borrowed from the British government by the Humber Bridge Board. To help pay for the bridge, drivers pay a toll, or fee, to cross. Most large suspension bridges in the world are toll bridges.

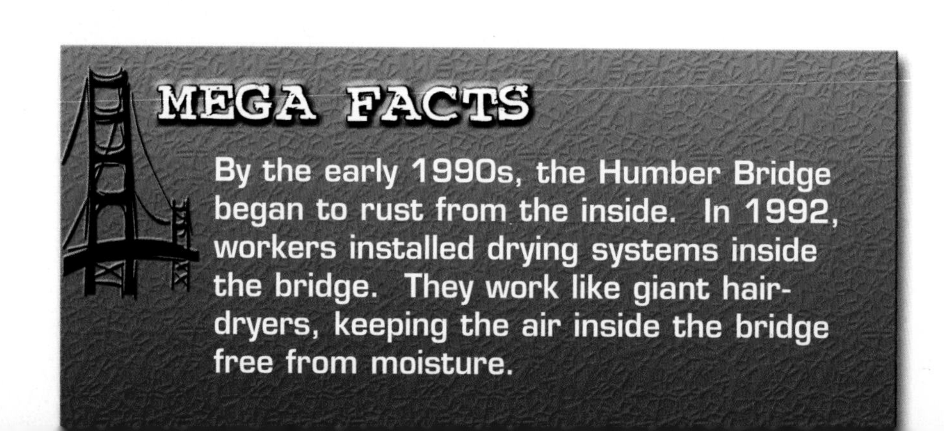

The Humber Bridge is not expected to be paid for until the year 2032. Bridge officials believe, however, that the benefits of improved travel and trade because of the bridge are worth its huge cost.

Humber Bridge officials estimate that the bridge will last for 120 years.

Lighting the Humber

The latest challenge for the Humber Bridge has to do with lighting. All of the world's ten longest bridges have lights at night — except for the Humber. Although there have been plans to light up the bridge, none have been completed.

Some environmental groups worry that the bright lights will interrupt the breeding of birds that live near the Humber Estuary. Hundreds of thousands of birds migrate along the estuary each year, and the lights might also keep them from flying up the river. To prevent these problems, bridge officials are experimenting with laser lights on the main cables. These lights would reflect off special paint on the bridge. Officials think these special lights will reduce the glare of light in the sky and surrounding areas and will use less energy.

CHAPTER 4

AMAZING CONNECTIONS

The second longest bridge span in the world is really one part of a combination of bridges and tunnels. In Denmark, the entire 4-mile- (6-km-) long Great Belt Fixed Link is split into three parts. It has a West Bridge and a railway tunnel. The Great Belt East Bridge, however, is the star of Denmark. It is a suspension bridge with a main span that measures 5,328 feet (1,624 m) – more than 1 mile (1.6 km)!

Denmark officials decided to build a link between Denmark and Sweden in 1986. It would take a system of several bridges and tunnels to connect the many islands of Denmark together and then to Sweden. Before the Great Belt Fixed Link, travel and trade between parts of Denmark were slow. The only way to get between the islands or to Sweden was by ferry, which took a very long time.

The West Bridge would connect the island of Funen with the tiny island of Sprogo. The Great Belt

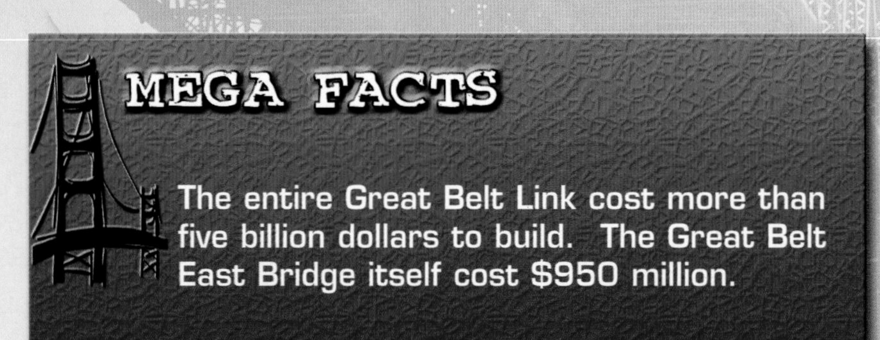

MEGA FACTS

The entire Great Belt Link cost more than five billion dollars to build. The Great Belt East Bridge itself cost $950 million.

This floating pontoon bridge crosses the Ganges River in India.

East Bridge would connect Sprogo Island and the island of Zealand. The bridges would also be the first links between the capital city of Copenhagen, in Zealand, and western Denmark. The construction project would be one of the biggest and most important in Denmark's history.

Construction on the Great Belt East Bridge began in 1991. Two

Float On

Pontoon bridges are special bridges that float. They are not permanently anchored like other types of bridges. Military groups often used pontoon bridges for temporary crossings during wars. The troops, or soldiers, could easily move the floating bridges into place on a river. After crossing the water, the troops could quickly take them apart.

Not all pontoon bridges are temporary. Some pontoon bridges are permanent and used for everyday traffic. The longest full-time pontoon bridge is in Seattle, Washington. The Evergreen Point Bridge opened in 1963. Its floating section spans more than 7,500 feet (2,286 m).

Oresund Cable-stayed Bridge

The final link between Denmark and the rest of Europe is the Oresund. It connects Denmark's capital city, Copenhagen, with Sweden. Like the Great Belt Link, it is a combination of bridges and a tunnel. Instead of a suspension bridge, however, one section of the Oresund is a cable-stayed bridge.

On a suspension bridge, cables support the deck. They transfer weight to concrete anchorages. On cable-stayed bridges, the cables support the entire weight of the deck themselves. Long steel cables come directly off the tower. They are stretched diagonally down to the bridge deck. When all the cables are in place, they look like the triangular sail of a huge sailboat.

The Oresund Bridge has a 1,607-foot (490-m) cable-stayed span. The longest cable-stayed span belongs to the Tatara Bridge in Japan. It is 2,919 feet (890 m) long.

different construction companies handled the project. One company built the towers and anchorages. First, workers built 833-foot- (254-m-) tall concrete towers. Next, they built two 358,248-ton (325,000-tonne) "A"-shaped concrete anchorages. The Great Belt East Bridge is the longest suspension bridge with both towers and anchorages built completely in the water. Most bridges have anchorages that are at least partly connected to the land along the water's edge.

The giant deck sections of the Great Belt East Bridge were

The Oresund Bridge carries both road and railway traffic.

built at another location. Each deck section looked like a 157-foot- (48-m-) long box. Barges shipped the sections to the bridge construction site. Cranes floating on barges lifted each section into place. Then workers welded the suspension boxes to girders, or beams, for additional support. To make sure the ends of each deck section fit with the next, workers matched up each end of the boxes as they were being built.

Forever in Second Place

On July 6, 1996, workers began spinning the cables that would support the bridge deck. They guided a large

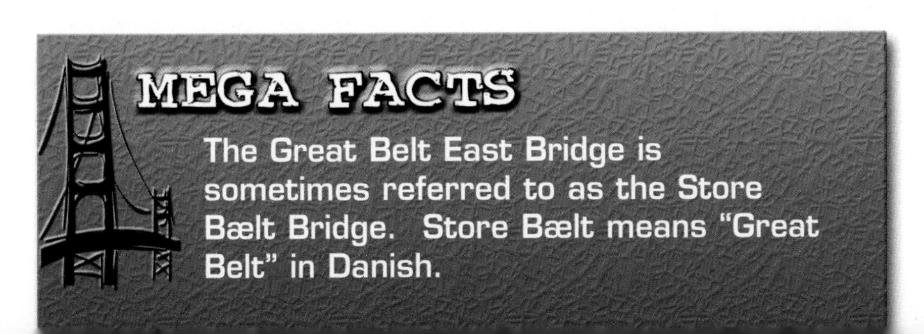

MEGA FACTS

The Great Belt East Bridge is sometimes referred to as the Store Bælt Bridge. Store Bælt means "Great Belt" in Danish.

spinning wheel above the bridge towers. The automated spinning wheel carried two loops of steel wire back and forth between the anchorages of the Great Belt East Bridge. They spun 10,102 feet (3,079 m) of steel wire into strands that would later be squeezed together to form the main cables. Each cable had thirty-seven strands, and each strand was made up of 504 steel wires. The spinning wheels worked through the summer months.

When October arrived in Denmark, so did raging storms. During one storm, winds reached more than 33 miles (53 km) per hour. At one point, wind gusts as strong as 45 miles (72 km) an hour pounded the bridge. The spinning wheels kept on working, however. The bridge was unharmed. Once the cables were finished, they contained 21,697 tons (19,683 tonnes) of steel wire. In all, the spinning wheels made 4,662 trips across the towers.

The Great Belt East Bridge opened for traffic on June 14, 1998. It never had the chance to win the title of world's longest bridge, however. In April of that same year, a longer bridge opened in Japan.

MEGA FACTS

In 2005, more than 25,000 vehicles crossed the Great Belt Link each day. The traffic is more than three times the number of cars that used to cross on the ferry before the bridge was built.

CHAPTER 5

OVER DANGEROUS WATERS

The Akashi Kaikyo stretches across an extremely wide body of water in Japan. The Akashi Strait is more than 2 miles (3 km) across! Its rushing waters are very dangerous. Currents in the strait often race at more than 10 miles (16 km) per hour.

In 1988, workers began digging the foundations for the bridge's massive towers in the waters of the Akashi Strait. Fast currents made digging dangerous and slow. Giant cranes lowered huge buckets to dig through the floor of the strait. Remote controlled cameras helped workers supervise the buckets underwater.

The designers of this bridge had enormous steel caissons built. Caissons are huge, watertight structures used in underwater construction. Each one is shaped like a large steel tube. Workers filled these tubes with both water-resistant concrete and steel reinforced concrete. The caissons of the Akashi Kaikyo were as tall as a twenty-one story building. They weighed more than 15,000 tons (13,600 tonnes). These caissons became the anchors for the giant bridge towers.

Akashi Innovations

Engineers had more than rough currents to think about

The Akashi Kaikyo is covered with more than 1,700 lights. They can be lit in at least twenty-eight different colors and patterns.

when they designed the Akashi Kaikyo. They also had to worry about huge tropical storms called typhoons. Like hurricanes, typhoons produce strong winds and high waves. Japan also gets severe earthquakes. The 927-foot (283-m) towers had to be able to move in the wind, but resist the violent shake of an earthquake.

Bridge designers decided to use devices called tuned mass dampers (TMD). TMDs are blocks of

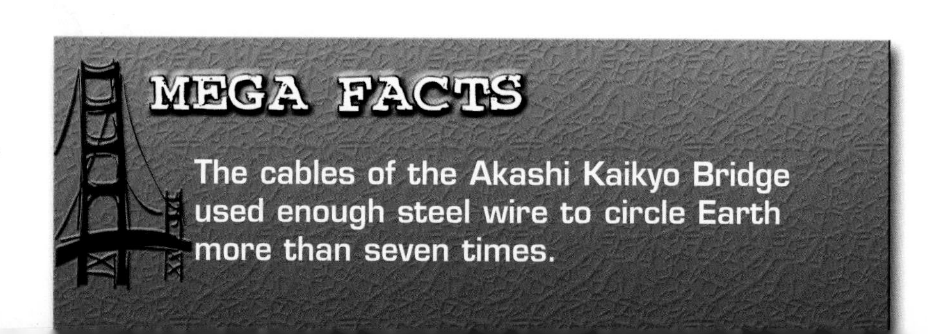

MEGA FACTS

The cables of the Akashi Kaikyo Bridge used enough steel wire to circle Earth more than seven times.

concrete weighing 10 tons (9 tonnes) each that hang inside the towers. Twenty TMDs are located throughout the inside of each tower. They work like pendulums. When the tower moves in one direction, the TMDs swing just enough in the other direction to bring the tower upright.

Unlike most suspension bridges, no machine or worker spun the cables of the Akashi Kaikyo at the bridge. Workers at another location bundled steel into 290 strands and shipped them to the bridge. Putting the cables in place, however, was difficult. The waters were too rough for a boat to haul a pilot rope from one anchorage to the other. Pilot ropes are temporary guide cables that stretch across the tops of the towers. They allow the main cables to be put into the correct place. Engineers decided to build a lighter pilot rope from the same strong material used to make bullet-proof vests. This material made the pilot rope lightweight enough to be flown into place by a helicopter.

Wind Tunnels

Super-long suspension bridges must be extra strong. To make sure the bridges are tough enough to handle any weather condition, engineers test the bridges before they are built. Engineers build scale models of the bridge. They test the models in giant wind tunnels.

Inside the wind tunnels, wind speeds can reach speeds of more than 100 miles (161 km) per hour. Engineers look at the sway, or movement, of the model bridge. The bridge has to move just enough without shaking itself to pieces.

Disaster Strikes

The Akashi Kaikyo Bridge's ability to survive a massive earthquake was tested before the bridge was finished. At 5:46 a.m. on January 17, 1995, a violent earthquake struck Kobe, Japan. It measured a staggering 7.2 on the Richter scale.

The quake destroyed buildings and killed more than five thousand people. The destruction was widespread. One of the few structures unharmed in the quake was the Akashi Kaikyo. The only change was to the length of the bridge. The designers had to increase the planned length of the Akashi Kaikyo because the earthquake had made the strait 3 feet (1 m) wider!

Once the pilot rope was in place, workers used wheels and pulleys to guide each of the 290 steel strands into position across the towers. Then they used a special machine to squeeze the strands so tightly that they formed one giant cable. When finished, the main cables were almost 4 feet (1.2 m) wide. All the cables were in place by the end of 1994.

Temporary Title

After workers built the towers and strung the cables, cranes lifted the massive deck into place. Bridge designers planned the deck with special steel plates called vertical

Heavy machinery breaks up the concrete rubble of a freeway that was knocked over by the 1995 earthquake in Kobe, Japan.

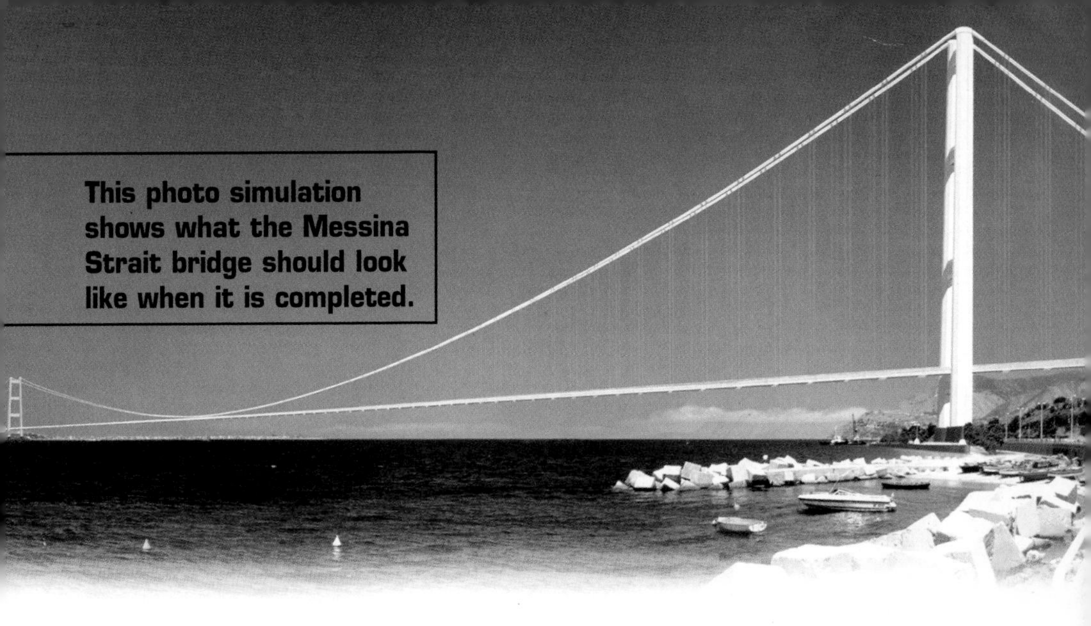

This photo simulation shows what the Messina Strait bridge should look like when it is completed.

stabilizers. Located in several places along the underside of the bridge deck, the stabilizers work like the tail of an airplane. They help balance changes in the air pressure around the bridge deck.

On April 5, 1998, the Akashi Kaikyo was opened to traffic. Its main span reaches an amazing 6,532 feet (1,991 m) long. Driving across the bridge has its price, however. Like most long bridges, drivers have to pay a toll. In 2006, it cost $23.00 to drive a medium-sized car across the "World's Longest Bridge".

It will not be long until another bridge pushes the Akashi Kaikyo to second place on the list of world's longest bridges. Engineers are already building and planning much longer structures. When finished in 2010, the main span of the Messina Strait Bridge, in Italy, will stretch 2 miles (3 km) long.

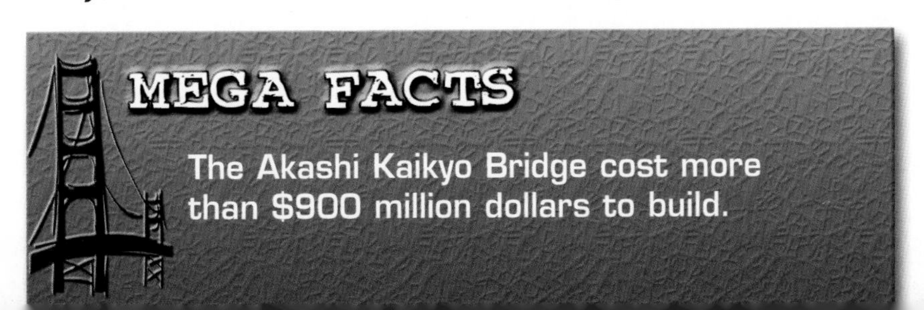

MEGA FACTS

The Akashi Kaikyo Bridge cost more than $900 million dollars to build.

TIME LINE

1937 The Golden Gate Bridge is completed. It has a main span of 4,200 feet (1,280 m).

1940 The Tacoma-Narrows Bridge collapses.

1951 A new, stronger Tacoma-Narrows Bridge is built

1964 The Verrazano-Narrows is completed in New York. It becomes the longest bridge in the United States. Its main span is only 60 feet (18 m) longer than the Golden Gate.

1981 The Humber Bridge is opened in Great Britain. Its main span stretches 4,626 feet (1,410 m) long.

1988 Construction begins on the Akashi Kaikyo Bridge in Japan.

1991 Construction begins on the Great Belt East Bridge in Denmark.

1995 Kobe, Japan, is hit by a disastrous earthquake. The Akashi Kaikyo survives unharmed.

1998 The Akashi Kaikyo is completed in April. It becomes the current "World's Longest Bridge" with a span measuring 6,532 feet (1,991 m). In June, the Great Belt East Bridge is completed. It comes in as the second-longest bridge with a span of 5,328 feet (1,624 m).

2000 Construction begins on the Messina Strait Bridge in Sicily.

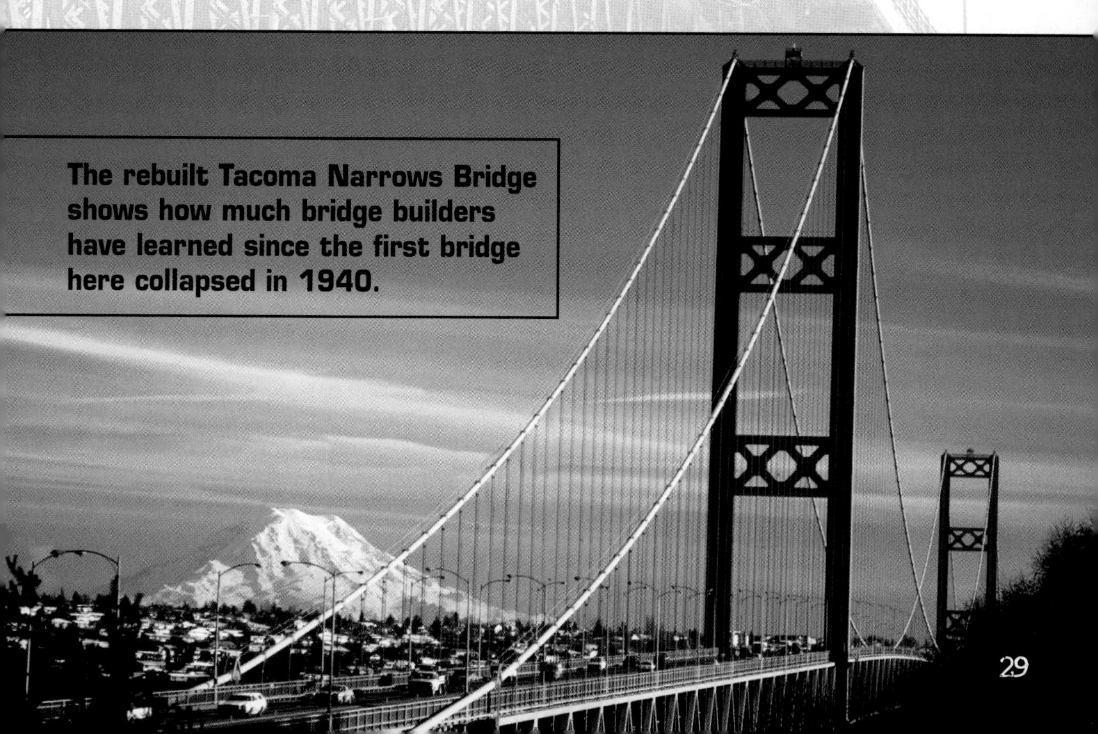

The rebuilt Tacoma Narrows Bridge shows how much bridge builders have learned since the first bridge here collapsed in 1940.

GLOSSARY

anchorages – massive concrete structures to which the cables of a suspension bridge are secured. Natural rock or cliffs can also serve as anchorages.

deck – a bridge's flat surface on which vehicles, people, and trains travel

detonator – a device used to set off explosives

engineer – someone who uses scientific knowledge to design and build bridges, roads, tunnels, and buildings

estuary – the lower part of a river where river and ocean currents meet, creating a mix of fresh and salt water

geology – the study of the earth's rock layers

girders – horizontal supports on a bridge

hangers – vertical cables on a suspension bridge that hang between the main cables and the bridge deck. They are also called suspender cables.

lawsuits – claims or complaints accusing someone of breaking the law and brought before a court of law

piers – vertical support structures under the spans of a bridge

pilot rope – a temporary cable that stretches across the top of the tower from one anchorage to the other. A pilot rope helps the main cables to be put in place.

Richter scale – a scale from 0 to 9 that measures the intensity of an earthquake, with 9 being the most severe

scale models – exact copies of structures that are much smaller in size

spans – the distances of a bridge between two supports

strait – a narrow passage of water connecting two larger bodies of water

toll – money a driver must pay to drive on a road

typhoons – hurricanes in the western Pacific Ocean

TO FIND OUT MORE

Books

Bridges. Transport and Communication (series). Melinda Farbman (Enslow Publishers, Inc.)

Bridges! Amazing Structures to Design, Build, and Test. Carol A. Johman and Elizabeth J. Reith (Williamson Publishing)

The Golden Gate Bridge. Cornerstones of Freedom (series). Sharlene and Ted Nelson (Children's Press)

The Longest Bridge. Extreme Places (series). Darv Johnson (Kidhaven Press)

Video

Building Big: Bridges (WGBH) NR

Web Sites

Bridges
www.bridgepros.com
Information on several long bridges and how to build bridges

Building Big
www.pbs.org/wgbh/buildingbig/bridge/index.html
PBS site with information on kinds of bridges and famous bridges

World's Longest Bridge Spans
www.tkk.fi/Units/Bridge/longspan.html
Lists of the longest bridges by type

Publisher's note to educators and parents: Our editors have carefully reviewed these Web sites to ensure that they are suitable for children. Many Web sites change frequently, however, and we cannot guarantee that a site's future contents will continue to meet our high standards of quality and educational value. Be advised that children should be closely supervised whenever they access the Internet.

INDEX

About the Author

Susan K. Mitchell lives near Houston, Texas. She is a teacher and the author of several picture books. Susan has also written many non-fiction books for kids. She has a wonderful husband, two daughters, a dog, two cats, and a pet squirrel. She dedicates this book to her in-laws, Fred and Patti.